Literacy Outdoors
50 Exciting Starting Points for Outdoor Literacy Experiences

<u>ACKNOWLEDGEMENTS</u>

Written by: Ros Bayley, Helen Bromley & Lynn Broadbent

Illustrated by: Peter Scott

Produced by: Lynda Lawrence

Published by: Lawrence Educational
PO Box 532, Cambridge, CB1 0BX, UK

© Lawrence Educational 2006

ISBN: 978-1-903670-53-8

Introduction

'The best classroom and the richest cupboard is roofed only by the sky' Margaret McMillan

In recent years there has been considerable emphasis on providing literacy experiences outside and when we reflect upon this in the context of child development it makes massive sense. Pause for a moment and think about all the things you enjoyed doing when you were very young, and the chances are, most of them were outside: children thrive on outdoor experiences and the importance cannot be overstated, especially for boys!

For children who spend large periods of time outside, it is essential that we make our outdoor areas exciting, literate environments. If we fail to do this, children will miss out on a whole range of experiences that are vital for their literacy development.

Literacy Outdoors aims to provide practical help in creating exciting and literate outdoor spaces. It focuses on:

- what we might provide
- how to provide literacy experiences through outside role-play activities
- how story can be used to enhance literacy experiences outside

These activities are only a starting point and we are sure that you will combine them with a wide range of your own ideas. We hope you will find the book useful and that you and the children will have fun trying out the ideas.

Ros Bayley, Helen Bromley & Lynn Broadbent

Contents

ACTIVITY 1

The Authors' and Illustrators' Toolkit

What you need:
A plastic toolbox with a handle (the kind with a variety of compartments and a snap down lid is best).
Pens, post it notes, string, sellotape, envelopes, postcards, writing paper, scissors, spiral bound notebooks, etc.

What you do:
Put the writing and illustrating equipment into the toolbox. Explain to the children that they can use it to draw and write outside and transport it to wherever they choose. Make clipboards available so that it is easy for the children to write anywhere and everywhere.
It is highly likely that you will need more than one toolkit, as children enjoy being able to write in a special place of their choice.
If you set up an adult initiated activity outside where you make a book with the children, they are usually very keen to do this for themselves afterwards. This activity will also give you the opportunity to model what illustrators do.

Further possibilities:
Add other special things to keep interest going and stimulate further ideas, for example glitter pens, dark paper and chalk, charcoal etc.
Add a selection of ready-made small books to the kit, to motivate the children even more.
Allow them to make their own decisions about the content of their books.
Be aware of their current interests and how they could be used as a basis for their books.
Introduce a camera and talk with them about how they could use photographs to illustrate their books.

Outdoor Writing Areas

What you need:
Resources for an outdoor writing area can range from the sublime to the ridiculous. If you are lucky enough to have a shed or an outdoor play house, why not turn it into a 'writing shed.' If this is not a possibility for you, buy some pop up tents or make a writing den out of an old clothes horse and a blanket.

What you do:
Resource your writing den in pretty much the same way as you would an indoor writing area. Include: paper in assorted colours, sizes and shapes; stationary and envelopes; pens, pencils, felt tip pens and crayons; scissors, stapler, hole punch, glue stick, message board, telephone, note pads, clipboards, labels, greetings cards, ready made books, split pins, elastic bands, etc. If your writing den is not a permanent structure, store these items in a large plastic box that can be easily transferred from inside to out. Hold a special 'launching party' for the writing area. This will give it value and provide you with an opportunity to introduce the children to the resources and how they can be used. Involve the children in drawing up ground rules for how the area should be used.

Further possibilities:
Encourage practitioners to spend some time in the writing area carrying out some writing of their own, for example, some planning, or writing up some observations, or even writing a story or a poem. Nobody will get much done but it will provide a marvellous opportunity for talking to the children about writing. Hold some special events in the writing den, for example, card making or book making sessions.

Chalk and Talk

What you need:
Some playground chalks.
Spaces for the children to draw, mark make and write. This might be the pavement, playground, or specially prepared boards painted with blackboard paint.

What you do:
Encourage the children to use the chalks outdoors for a variety of child and adult initiated activities. These might include pattern making, drawing and writing. Show the children how to mark-make using both their right and left hands. This will support right/left brain integration and help develop the manipulative skills necessary for later work in handwriting.

Literacy achievements realised outside should have equal status with those achieved indoors. Have a camera at the ready to record significant achievements that can be shared with others, such photographs can make valuable contributions to children's records of achievement

Further possibilities:
Work with the children to design a variety of games that can be chalked on to the playground or blackboards. Painting a board with magnetic paint will mean that the children can create magnetic pieces to use in their games.
Show the children pictures and photographs of street artists at work and encourage them to put in as much detail into their pavement art as possible. As you talk with them about their drawing you will really help to develop their narrative skills. Drawing in this way will also help to develop the visual discrimination for later work in handwriting.

Posters, Posters, Everywhere!

What you need:

Some posters, pictures or charts depicting wild birds, minibeasts, trees and flowers.
Collect together some favourite raps, poems, songs and action rhymes, and print them out on large sheets.
You might also add some printed instructions for playing different games.
A laminator. Once laminated the posters can be displayed in the outside area.

What you do:

Share the posters with the children and encourage them to offer their ideas for the best places to display them. Talk with them about how the posters can be used and hold some adult initiated sessions to demonstrate their use. For many young children print is invisible and it is not until we draw their attention to it and give it status that it has meaning for them!

Further possibilities:

When favourite picture books fall apart turn them into posters and display them outside for outside story reading sessions. (You will obviously need two copies of each book!)
Link this activity to your Authors and Illustrators Toolkit and support the children to generate ideas for their own posters

A Performance Area

What you need:
This will depend upon whether you wish to create a permanent or a non-permanent performance area. For a permanent area you will need a raised platform, which may or may not have sides to it and some simple benches for the audience. For a non-permanent area you can simply 'zone off' part or your outside space and carry chairs out from indoors, or provide a blanket or mats for the audience to sit on.
Provide props and dressing-up clothes to stimulate the children's imaginations.
You may also like to provide a cassette player and some favourite music and story CD's

What you do:
Young children learn by listening watching and copying so model some of the many ways in which this area can be used. Get all the adults together and perform the Three Little Pigs or the Three Billy Goats Gruff for the children. Once they have seen you do it they will be sure to want to try it for themselves. Invite individuals or groups of children to perform their favourite songs or role play their favourite stories. Have an adult based in the performance area to act as the storyteller and 'scaffold' the children's performances.

Further possibilities:
Invite guests to perform for the children in the special area. This could include older children, parents or other adults from the local community. Once a special performance has been arranged, post up the details of the events giving times, dates and names and draw the children's attention to the forthcoming attractions. If particular groups of children have worked hard on a performance, have a group of invited guests to be an audience for an extra special event.

Long Handled Brushes

What you need:
Some cheap decorator's brushes.
Broom handles.
Gaffer tape or screws.
Plastic containers and water.

What you do:
Saw the broom handles in half and smooth off any rough edges with sandpaper. Screw or bind the decorator's brushes to the half broom handles. Good handwriting comes from the shoulder and playing with long handled brushes is excellent for developing fluid movement. Show the children how to use the brushes on a patch or concrete or some paving slabs. Be prepared for the fact that they will initially just want to paint everything. It is really important to let them work through this stage, after which you can model and suggest a range of pattern making, drawing and writing activities.

Further possibilities:
Mix up some paint and let the children mark-make on the reverse side of some unwanted rolls of wallpaper. Try adding glitter or glue to the paint and once the children have painted the paper, supply wide toothed combs etc. with which they can extend their mark-making.

Alphabet Boxes

What you need:
Plastic or wooden containers. (These can be glued or screwed into place as a permanent fixture or simply taken outside as and when required). They can range in size from margarine tubs to large plastic containers.
A selection of artefacts, e.g. small world toys such as vehicles, animals, small toys and teddies etc.

What you do:
Hide your collection of artefacts all over the outside area. Explain to the children that there are all sorts of things hidden under stones, in the branches of trees, in the grass and in the flowers, on window ledges etc. Further explain that as each item is found it is to be stored according to initial sound, then let the hunt begin! (For some children it may be helpful to provide photographs of the items that have been hidden so that they know what they are searching for).

Further possibilities:
Use your boxes to store resources for the children to access materials from, for example, clipboards in the 'c' box and balls in the 'b' box etc. When the children have finished with the materials encourage then to return them to the appropriate box.

Washing Lines

What you need:
String and pegs (and cup hooks, if there are no suitable places for tying up your string).
Laminated letters.

What you do:
Make a washing line at a suitable height for the children and model how to use the pegs and laminated letters to make words and simple sentences for messages. The children might like to use the letters to make their names or you could peg up the alphabet, leaving gaps for them to fill.

Further possibilities:
Cut out and laminate pages from worn out picture books. (You will need two of each book.) The children can peg up the cards in the correct sequence and tell the story for themselves.
You or the children could also photograph a sequence of events, which could then be laminated and used in a similar way.
Leave messages or notes on the washing line for the children to find each day. This will promote discussion and create situations that the children can make a written response to.

ACTIVITY 9

Blackboards, Whiteboards, Flipcharts and Slates

What you need:
As the title suggests you will need a variety of different writing surfaces and the appropriate markers.

What you do:
If you have any old blackboards in your setting why not screw these to the walls. They make excellent surfaces for drawing, mark making and writing messages. Similarly, using a flipchart or painting easel for message writing, scoring for games or a place where children can 'sign up' for activities. Provide smaller whiteboards or slates for individual use. Model how the resources can be used for a wide variety of purposes.

Further possibilities:
Invite specific people in the setting and from the local community, to leave 'special messages' for the children.
Start an interactive message board. Write a message to which the children can make a response. You can then respond to their message and the activity can extend until it reaches a natural conclusion. Encourage the children to leave messages for each other. You might even leave messages from fictional characters, for example a giant, a fairy or an alien.

A Book Den

What you need:
A pop-up tent, or a three sided frame and a large blanket or drape. (An old fashioned clothes horse is ideal for this purpose.)

What you do:
Once you have made your structure, fill it with some exciting fiction and non-fiction picture books. To launch your book den hold a special story reading and storytelling ceremony.
A book den is a great resource for children who spend a lot of time outside and can make a cosy retreat that can be used between more vigorous activities. Put an easel or whiteboard outside the book den with a timetable for story sessions.

Further possibilities:
Make your book den as dark as possible using extra thick drapes, and hold story sessions by torchlight. Hold some storytelling sessions around particular themes, for example animal stories, dinosaur stories or stories by a particular author.

A Steady Beat Station

Because a sense of steady beat underpins our ability to pick up the patterns of sound in language it is essential that we help young children to develop this skill – and a steady beat station can really help!

What you need:
A variety of plastic bowls, buckets and plates.
Old saucepans and saucepan lids.
Wooden spoons, washing up mops and chop sticks.
Some strong string or twine.

What you do:
Place the buckets, saucepans, bowls and plates upside down on the floor. If you have some low tables available – even better! Suspend the string between two poles or tie it to a fence. Tie the saucepan lids to the string. (You may well have some other sound-makers you wish to add to the string). Tie off the ends of the washing up mops to make them into beaters. (You can also secure them with a strong elastic band). Show the children how the various beaters will make a variety of sounds and the let them explore and experiment for themselves. Encourage them to notice and describe the various sounds that they make.

Further possibilities:
Add a CD player and some music with a strong, steady beat to your steady beat area. Encourage the children to select their favourite pieces of music and 'drum away' to the beat.

Puppet Fun

What you need:

A simple structure to act as a 'play board.' (This could be as simple as a large cardboard box with a hole cut in it or you may find it worth while to invest in a more permanent wooden structure that can be used as a puppet theatre).

A collection of finger puppets and glove puppets.

Materials with which the children can make their own puppets, for example, paper plates, wooden spoons old socks and gloves, glue, felt tipped pens, wool etc.

A CD player and some CD's of traditional tales.

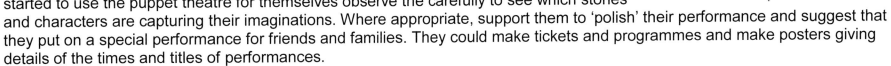

What you do:

Talk with the children about all the different ways in which the puppet theatre could be used, and if possible, get the adults in the setting to perform some simple puppet plays for the children. If children race about hitting each other over the head with puppets it is invariably because they are unsure about how to use them. If they have seen adults model the use of puppets, and if the adults involve themselves in the activity, where appropriate, the children are usually very keen to have a go themselves. Ask the children if they have any favourite stories that they would like to see acted out as a puppet show. Once the children have started to use the puppet theatre for themselves observe the carefully to see which stories and characters are capturing their imaginations. Where appropriate, support them to 'polish' their performance and suggest that they put on a special performance for friends and families. They could make tickets and programmes and make posters giving details of the times and titles of performances.

Further possibilities:

Try making some really large puppets which can be operated by several children working together. For example, a dragon, a dinosaur or a monster. These can be made really simply using cardboard boxes, drapes and gaffer tape and are excellent for stimulating the children's imaginations!

Treasure Hunt

What you need:
A small wooden or metal box, to use as a treasure chest.
Some treasure. (This could take the form of a small gift for each of the children, such as a pencil, rubber or similar small token.)

What you do:
Hide the treasure chest in an interesting place in the outside area. If you can, dig a hole and bury it underground; the children really like the idea of buried treasure! Write or draw a list of instructions that will eventually lead the children to the treasure. You could write a list of instructions and hide them in various places, for example: 'Go to the tree in the middle of the garden and look for a message tied to the branch.' There could be a further message leading them to the next clue and eventually to the treasure.

Further possibilities:
If you have a class puppet or a special toy or mascot, hide it in the outside area. Write a letter from the toy to the children giving some clues as to its location and see how long it takes them to find it.

Roll up!

What you need:
A selection of buckets of different sizes and colours, plastic and metal.
A variety of paint rollers and/or large paintbrushes.
Food colouring (optional)
Glitter (optional)
A good supply of water.
Space to paint.

What you do:
It is a really good idea to introduce this as an adult initiated activity. Show the children how to fill the buckets for themselves and talk with them about the materials available. Make a few suggestions for how and where the rollers and brushes can be used and then stand back and let the children explore the materials for themselves. Observe their mark-making and talk with them about their creations. Once you have done this leave the materials out during child initiated times so that the children can build on and extend the experience.

Further possibilities:
Make this activity available in all weathers so that the children can compare the changes that take place in the marks that they have made.

Wet Paper, Dry Paper

What you need:
A selection of large sheets of paper and card.
Paints, inks, chalks, felt pens.
Water and brushes.

What you do:
This is an excellent activity for promoting language for explaining, and although it can be done inside it is more effective outside where you do not have to worry about the mess.
Wet some of the paper and card with large brushes and water and leave some dry.
Let the children use the art materials on both sets of paper and card (wet and dry). Talk to them about the differences that they observe in how the marks are made. Encourage them to compare the two sets of drawings.

Further possibilities:
If weather permits, set up an art gallery outside so that they can all admire each other's artwork.

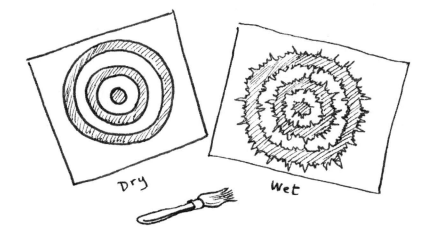

Ice Writing

What you need:
Some ice cube trays.
Food colouring.
Glitter.
Sheets of paper, plain and coloured.
A painting easel or similar.

What you do:
Freeze a selection of ice cubes. Leave some plain, but add a variety of food colourings and/or glitter to others. Remove them from the trays when they are completely frozen. Put them outside with some large sheets of paper, clipped to an easel. Explain to the children that they are going to use the ice as writing utensils. Model some of the ways in which this can be done and then let the children explore the materials for themselves. Talk with them about the marks they make, encouraging language for observation, analysis and explanation.

Further possibilities:
Freeze some plain water 'ice lollies' with sticks, for a different mark making experience.
Encourage the children to generate their own ideas about what might be added to the water to make ice-writing materials.

Outdoor Alphabets

What you need:
An outdoor environment and some children.
A camera.
A laminating machine.

What you do:
Start by talking about your indoor alphabet poster/frieze and then explain to the children that you would like to make one for the outside area. Encourage them to think of, and find things in the outdoor environment that begin with each letter of the alphabet. This is much easier if you don't restrict the words to nouns. For example, include actions such as jumping, climbing, and bouncing.

Make a large chart showing each of the letters of the alphabet, with space to add ideas as they are collected. Don't worry about missing letters.

Plan the taking of the photographs with the children. When they have been taken, print them off (A4 is a good size) and laminate them. If you have a suitable surface outdoors then you can display the alphabet outside.

Further possibilities:
Make more than one copy of the pictures so that you can make a matching alphabet book for use indoors and out.

Talking Technology

What you need:
At least one sound recording device that can be used easily outside. Digital voice recorders are particularly valuable as children's recordings can be uploaded onto a computer.

What you do:
Work with small groups initially to show the children how to use the recording equipment for themselves. Then allow them to experiment with recording the sounds that they hear outside. Encourage the children to listen for the widest variety of sounds possible. Play the sounds back to the children so that they can revisit their 'journey' around the outdoor area. Can they identify where and how the different noises were made?

Further possibilities:
Use the recording equipment to record playground songs and rhymes, musical performances, interviews, storytelling etc. Build up a bank of recordings that can be use in the indoor listening area.

For practitioners with well developed ICT skills, you could combine sound recordings with the photographs on a computer to create unique multimedia texts about the outdoor area.

Taking the Mike

What you need:
A variety of different types of pretend microphones, for example, echo mikes, musical mikes etc.

What you do:
Talk with the children about the materials to establish what they already know about microphones and how they are used. Make some suggestions for how and where the microphones could be used in the outside area. Put them where the children can access them freely. Encourage exploratory play. Observe the children carefully as they work with the microphones and involve yourself in the play where appropriate.

Further possibilities:
Provide a stage in the form of milk crates, or large construction equipment, or a TV screen made from a large cardboard box.
If you have some large sheets of fabric, find a place to hang them, so that the children can appear from behind the curtains, just like a real theatre.

A Little Squirt?

What you need:
A selection of empty washing up liquid bottles, with their nozzles.
Water.
Space.

What you do:
If practical, show the children how to fill the bottles themselves. Encourage them to squirt their patterns onto the space available. How far can they make the water go? What happens as the water in the bottle gets less? Can the children write their name before the bottle runs out of water?
Model a range of patterns and marks for the children to try out and then encourage them to think of patterns and marks of their own for you to try out!

Further possibilities:
Put out some plain paper – old rolls of wallpaper will do. Fill the bottles with thin paint or coloured ink. Use them to make patterns on the paper.
Obtain some pictures of the work of Jackson Pollock to show the children, and use for comparison. (You might be surprised at the similarities!!)

Down the Tubes

What you need:
A selection of tubes and pipes of various lengths. This might include cardboard tubes, hose, pipe lagging etc.

What you do:
This can be an excellent speaking and listening activity when well supported. Show the children how to use the various tubes as telephones and explore and talk about all the different sounds they can make. Encourage the children to articulate clearly and listen attentively as they communicate with one another. Discuss all the different ways in which the tubes might be used and supply the children with message pads and markers for writing down the messages they receive.

Further possibilities:
Add funnels to the collection of tubes and see how the noises change! Discuss the changes in sound with the children.
Incorporate the tubes into role - play areas and dens, so that children can devise their own uses for them.

Bubble Blowing

What you need:

A range of bubble blowing equipment. This could include a variety of blowers, a bubble making machine, etc.
A good supply of bubble liquid.

What you do:

Create an environment full of bubbles for the children to talk about and explore.
What do they notice?
How do they think the bubbles are made?
Make sure that you carry this activity out in a variety of weathers. Think about how the bubbles behave differently in sunshine, wind and rain. This is an excellent activity for promoting both descriptive language and language for thinking.
Take photographs to keep a record of the event.

Further possibilities:

Make some bubble prints, either in doors or out. Do this by mixing thin paint or ink and adding washing up liquid. Let the children blow through a straw to create bubbles and lay some paper across them. When dry use them for the children to write on.

Romp in the Swamp

What you need:
A copy of 'Romp in the Swamp' by Ian Whybrow, illus. By Adrian Reynolds.
A plastic laundry basket.
Some string.
Some diggers and trucks.
Some small world dinosaurs.
A length of hose.
Cushions or sheets of fabric.
Plant material, either real or artificial.

What you do:
Read the story with the children. If possible, have some multiple copies available so that children can re-visit it in small groups. Offer the children the selection of props suggested above, so that they can make their primordial swamp and snake trap outside, just like Harry and Charlie. They might want to first design their traps for Mr. Snakey, before making them.

Further possibilities:
Devise a Romp in the Swamp dance, and set it to music composed by the children. Perform it around the outdoor area! Photograph the dance as it happens and use the photographs to support the development of language for reporting. You may want to let the children caption the photographs so that they can be made into a book. You could also make a video that could be shared with friends and families.

The Gruffalo

What you need:
A copy of 'The Gruffalo', by Julia Donaldson.
Some ribbons, strips of fabric, wool, etc.
Clothes pegs would be useful, for attaching tails to waistbands.
Musical instruments.
Simple den building equipment, e.g. A frames and fabric dust sheets.

What you do:
After sharing the story with the children, work together to re-create the Gruffalo story outdoors. Discuss the characters in the book with the children and decide how very simple costumes can be made. This might be in the form of tails – from plaited ribbons or strips of material, masks made and designed by the children, or hats.
Devise sound effects to represent the different animals in the Gruffalo Story (Don't forget to include the Gruffalo himself). Re-enact the story with the children.
Build a den for The Gruffalo to inhabit and use it as a role-play area, so that children can create their own versions of the story for themselves.

Further possibilities:
Devise a Gruffalo dance, take photographs or video it! (Use in the same way as suggested for Romp in the Swamp.)

The Green Ship

What you need:
A copy of 'The Green Ship' by Quentin Blake.
An atlas.
A globe.
A telescope.
Junk materials to build with, including boxes, crates, rope, fabric, cardboard tubes, etc.

What you do:
After reading the story with the children, work together to build a ship from junk materials and/or large construction equipment.
Then, let the adventures begin! Add the globe and the atlas so that the children can plan their adventures. Make sure that children have access to other model making materials should they need to make more equipment for their ship.

Further possibilities:
Provide the children with a builder's tray (or similar container), some florists' oasis and some moss. Build the small scale Green Ship using the oasis. Add a family of small world people and support the children to extend the narrative.

Make a Ship's Log, by covering an unused exercise book or a diary with some interesting looking paper, so that children can make a note of their adventures and record sightings that they have made through the telescope.

Plan to have tea on the deck, just like the children in the book. Work with the children to make a list of what will be required and draw up a menu.

Come Away From the Water Shirley

What you need:
A copy of 'Come away from the Water Shirley' by John Burningham
Sand.
Water.
Small world pirate figures.
A small world family.

What you do:
Read the story with the children.
Set up a beach scene in a Builder's Tray and add the family and the pirates.
You could create a desert island with a box of treasure. This activity can
also be set up in a sand tray, compost tray or outdoor sandpit.
Let the children make up their own adventures for Shirley and her family.

Further possibilities:
If you have a large sand area outside, you could obtain some deckchairs so
that children could role-play the trip to the beach. Adding picnic equipment, buckets and spades and a newspaper will add to the
authenticity.

Take a series of photographs of the scenes that the children create to turn in to their very own 'Come Away From The Water'
book. Ensure that the children dictate the text for their book, to make it easy for them to be able to read it independently.

Owl Babies

What you need:

A copy of 'Owl Babies' by Martin Waddell published by Walker Books.
Some twigs and leaves and feathers.
Some toy owls – three babies if possible.
A letter to tuck into the nest (see below)

What you do:

Prior to this activity read the 'Owl Babies' story to the children.

Make a nest some where in the outdoor area, in a slightly secret place, where the children will discover it. Place the three baby owls there, along with a letter to the children. The letter may take a variety of forms. Perhaps it might be from the owl mother, asking the children to think of ways to amuse the baby owls whilst she is gone, or it could be from the baby owls themselves, asking the children if they know any good ways to prevent them being scared of the dark. When the letter has been discovered, read it with the children and decide how best to solve the problem. Encourage the children to write back to the owl mother or the owl babies, to offer them help and advice.

Further possibilities:

Create a dark den by using black or brown fabric draped over A frames or attached to garden canes, etc. Supply torches so that the children can explore the dark space that has been created.

Where's Julius?

What you need:
A copy of 'Where's Julius' by John Burningham
A place to dig.
Den building equipment.
An atlas and/or a globe.

What you do:
Read the story with the children. Discuss which of Julius' adventures they find most interesting. Which one would they most like to try? Offer them opportunities to explore as many of the scenarios as possible.

Further possibilities:
Add a diary to the role-play scenarios developed from the story so that the children can keep a record of all the adventures that they have. Adding a packet of blank postcards would also offer opportunities for writing.

Billy's Bucket

What you need:
A copy of 'Billy's Bucket' by Kes Gray and Garry Parsons.
A selection of buckets. This might include a buckets in a variety of sizes, materials and colours.
Access to a wide variety of underwater, small world toys.
Water.

What you do:
Read the story of Billy's Bucket to the children. Suggest that they create their own underwater world in a bucket, using found materials and the toys provided. Set aside some time so that children can share their stories with each other, and explain the contents of their particular bucket.

Further possibilities:
Write a song about the contents of the bucket, to the tune of 'The Wheels on The Bus.'
A sample verse might be:

> The crab in the bucket goes
> Nip nip nip,
> Nip nip nip,
> Nip nip nip,
> The crab in the bucket goes
> Nip nip nip,
> All day long …

Whatever Next

What you need:
A copy of 'Whatever Next!' by Jill Murphy
A large cardboard box.
A colander.
Some wellington boots.
Some food and drink (real or pretend).
A teddy bear.

What you do:
Share the story of Whatever Next! with the children and then introduce them to the role play materials and talk with them about how they could be used. Ask them if there is anything else they would like to add to the things that you have already collected. Once you have decided who is going and talked about what they might do when they get to moon you might help them to make up a rhyme for the countdown/blast-off. Once they get to the moon, observe their play carefully to see if you can extend it by adding extra resources.

Further possibilities:
Provide walkie talkies so that the children can radio home. Make up a 'moon dance' and video it. Write a diary of the children's adventures on the moon.

We're Going on a Bear Hunt

What you need:
A copy of 'We're Going on a Bear Hunt' by Michael Rosen and Helen Oxenbury
An expanse of grass.
Some blue material for a river.
Some brown material for thick, oozy mud.
Real or pretend trees for the forest.
White materials for the snow storm.
Den building materials for the cave.
A large teddy bear.
A blanket or opened out sleeping bag or duvet.

What you do:
Share the story with the children and introduce them to the collection
of materials you have gathered together for role-playing the story.
Talk with them about where the different things could be located and
lay out the materials in preparation for the Bear Hunt. Read the story
again, this time moving to the different locations as you read,
finishing up with everyone diving under the sleeping bag or duvet.
Record the story so that the children can listen to it again and role play it on their own.

Further possibilities:
Write your own story about a hunt, maybe a dinosaur hunt or a tiger hunt. Photograph it as it is role played and use the
photographs as a basis for a book.

Where the Wild Things Are

What you need:
A copy of 'Where the Wild Things Are' by Maurice Sendak.
Some construction equipment to make a boat.
Some materials for making 'wild thing' masks.
A pop up tent.
Some trees (if available)
Some musical instruments or 'wild' music.

What you do:
Share the story with the children and talk about how they could make the boat in which they could sail to the land of the wild things. Collect together a range of suitable construction equipment and support them to build a boat. Talk about the sort of noises the wild things might make and discuss the different ways in which they might move. Support the children to find suitable dressing up clothes and help them to make some 'wild things' masks. If you have any trees, plan a wild rumpus around them. Play some wild music to accompany the proceedings, or even better encourage the children to make their own music.

Further possibilities:
Photograph the children in their 'wild thing' costumes and use the photographs as a basis for a book about wild things. Get each child to describe their photograph and use their descriptions as captions for the photographs.

Duck in the Truck

What you need:
A copy of 'Duck in the Truck' by Jez Alborough.
A builder's tray.
Soil.
Water.
Stones and pebbles.
Small world animal figures – a duck, a frog, a sheep and a goat.
A small-world truck, jeep and boat.

What you do:
Share the story of 'Duck in the Truck' with the children and let them explore and talk about the collection of materials you have provided. Talk with them about what 'muck' is and how you can make it. Suggest that they could create their own 'muck/mud landscape' in the builder's tray, using the materials provided. Support the children to create the landscape and encourage them to refer to the pictures in the book. Read the story again and this time support the children to re-enact the story using the small world characters.

If this activity can be left out for some days the children will become more confident storytellers and also can be encouraged to add or adapt the landscape they have created.

Further possibilities:
Discuss with the children other things they could add to the landscape and other characters they could include in the story.

Photograph the process and support the children to create a book, with the children dictating the text to make it easier for them to be able to read it independently.

Run, Run as Fast as you Can

What you need:
Several versions of the story of 'The Gingerbread Man'.
Dressing up clothes.
Materials for making masks.
Labels for the various characters.
Blue material for the river.

What you do:
Over time share the stories with the children. Talk about the ways in which they are similar and the ways in which they are different. Let the children decide which characters they would like in their version of the story and make available suitable dressing up clothes and masks. Write out the names of the various characters on pieces of card. Punch holes in the card and thread string through the holes. (The children can wear the label for the character they are playing and they very quickly learn to read the names of all the rest of the characters!) This is an ideal story for outside as you can really go to town on the chase! Once everything is ready help the children to plan the route and have the various characters take up their positions ready for the chase.

Further possibilities:
Once the children have practiced the role play a few times and have built up their confidence, make your own video version of the Gingerbread Man for the children to take home and share with their families.

On the Bridge

What you need:
Various versions of the story of 'The Three Billy Goats Gruff'.
Suitable large construction materials for making a bridge.
Masks and dressing up clothes.

What you do:
Over time share the various versions of the story with the
children and encourage them to spot the similarities and
differences. Support them to sort out suitable costumes and
masks for the characters and also support them to role play the
story. In the first instance act as storyteller yourself
encouraging the children to add whatever dialogue they feel
confident to do. Teach them the popular rhymes that feature in
this story and make up some new ones of your own.

Further possibilities:
Make your own book about crossing the bridge. Take a photograph of every child crossing the bridge and talk with them about
why they may be crossing. Make a book using the photographs and caption each one with, for example 'Omar is crossing the
bridge to go shopping for a remote control car.'

Room on the Broom

What you need:
A copy of 'Room on the Broom' by Julia Donaldson.
A witch's broom or besom (they can be sourced on the internet).
A witch's cloak and hat.
Soft toy characters – a cat, a dog, a bird, a frog and a dragon.
String and sellotape to attach the toys to the broom.

What you do:
Share the story of 'Room on the Broom' with the children and then introduce them to the collection of materials you have gathered together for role-play. Ask them if there are other things that they would like to add to the collection.

Discuss the characters with the children and then support them to choose which characters they would like to role-play. They can either play all the characters themselves or use the soft toys you have provided. Read the story again and this time support the children to re-enact the story. Initially, you will need to act as storyteller and encourage the children to contribute their own dialogue.

If this activity is available for a few days the children will have the opportunity to become more confident as storytellers.

Further possibilities:
Provide broom handles, twigs and string, and support the children to make their own broom.
Provide materials and fabrics that the children can use to make cloaks, hats, etc.
Encourage the children to 'fly' in the outdoor area and devise their own adventures on their broom.
Take photographs of the children 'flying' on their brooms. Make a book using the photographs with the children providing the captions for the pictures.

The Garden Centre

What you need:
Flowerpots.
Seed packets.
Seed trays.
Wet and dry florists oasis for making flower arrangements.
Some artificial flowers.
Garden Books and Magazines.
Seed Catalogues.
Materials for making signs, price lists etc.
Compost, and trays.

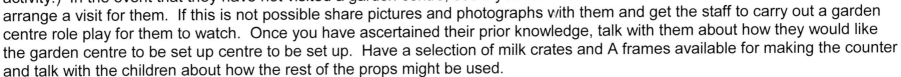

What you do:
Talk with the children to find out what they know about a garden centre.
(If this is not within their experience, they will not be able to role play the
activity.) In the event that they have not visited a garden centre, see if you can
arrange a visit for them. If this is not possible share pictures and photographs with them and get the staff to carry out a garden
centre role play for them to watch. Once you have ascertained their prior knowledge, talk with them about how they would like
the garden centre to be set up centre to be set up. Have a selection of milk crates and A frames available for making the counter
and talk with the children about how the rest of the props might be used.

Further possibilities:
Once the garden centre is established support the children to plant seeds in a variety of growing materials e.g. sand, compost,
newspaper etc. As the seeds grow, talk with the children about their observations, and record them on post-it notes that can be
put up for others to share.

The Drive Thru' Restaurant

What you need:
Wheeled vehicles.
Some simple equipment to make a counter (cardboard boxes, milk crates etc.)
Plates, cups, etc
Clipboards.
Some menus, preferably made with the children.
Aprons and hats would enhance the role-play, but are not essential.
Litter bins!

What you do:
Discuss the setting up of the restaurant with the children. Use their prior knowledge of drive thru's and ensure that you incorporate their ideas in your planning.
Talk with the children about how the wheeled toys will gain access to the restaurant. Supply chalk and cones so that they can experiment with the lay-out until they achieve one they are happy with. Talk with the children about what signs and symbols will be needed. Plan an area where take-away meals can be eaten once they have been purchased.

Further possibilities:
Observe the children carefully as they play in the restaurant. Be aware of how they are using the restaurant and how you might extend and build o this. For example you may want to provide telephones and start deliveries.

The Garage Mechanic

What you need:

A selection of replica and real spanners, screwdrivers, oil cans etc
Clipboards.
Some photocopied MOT certificates.
An appointments book.
Some forms for recording 'work done', parts used, etc
A good range of car and motorbike magazines.
At least one Haynes car manual, (the more the better).
Pens, pencils.

What you do:

Talk with the children to find out what they know about garages and how they operate. If possible arrange a visit to a local garage. If not show them pictures, posters and videos.
Organise part of the outdoor area to be set-aside for Vehicle Repairs. Provide milk-crates, ropes and planks and talk with the children about how they would like the garage to be set up. Discuss what services will be offered and support the children to make signs giving details of opening hours etc.

Further possibilities:

Add car washing to the facilities offered by the garage, to offer opportunities for large-scale water play. The large sweeping movements needed for washing cars are also excellent for developing the manipulative skills necessary for writing.

The Pirate Box

What you need:
Eye patches.
Curtain rings.
Scraps of fabric for headscarves.
Cardboard Tubes to make telescopes, etc
Some simple pirate hats.
Old coins.
A box for treasure.
A parrot puppet.

What you do:
Prior to introducing the Pirate Box to the children, set the context by reading or telling some pirate stories. You may also have some video material you could share with them. Let them explore the contents of the box and talk with the children about what the items are for and how they could be used. Use the box in conjunction with some large construction equipment and talk with the children about how they could use it to make a pirate ship. As you observe the children at play, look out for opportunities to make treasure maps, flags and signs.

Further possibilities:
If you have large-scale sand provision outside, then bury some coins, keys, etc in it and let the children use simple metal detectors to discover the treasure. Alternatively, use a paddling pool full of sand for the same purpose.

The Magic Garden Box

What you need:

Some sheets of attractive fabric, e.g. net, gauze, organza, etc.
Some sheets of black fabric.
Some clips and pegs.
Some magic wands.
A toy frog.
A garden gnome or two.
Some wooden toadstools (not essential, but add atmosphere).
A small plastic cauldron would be useful, but is not essential. The sort sold as plant containers are ideal.

What you do:

Prior to introducing the children to the box it is really beneficial to share some stories about gnomes, fairies and other magical creatures with them. You may even consider setting up a provocation. For example, make a fairy ring and leave an interesting object in the middle of it. This could be a magic ring or little treasure chest. Talk with the children about who may have left it there. Then offer the contents of the box to the children and encourage them to invent their own magical characters, using the props available.

Help them combine the fabrics to make costumes. Teach them tying and fixing techniques, but avoid dominating their choice of outfits!

Further possibilities:

Add some attractive writing implements to the box – gel pens, brightly coloured paper, etc, so that children can write magic messages and create their own spells.
Use large sheets of magical looking fabric to create a den, where all the enchanted characters can live.

The Archaeologist's Box

What you need:
Some interesting old pieces of broken pottery.
Some old bones (These can be acquired from the butcher and once thoroughly cleaned, boiled and disinfected are great for this activity).
Some interesting looking stones, 'jewels' or fossils.
Some trowels and brushes.
Magnifying glasses.
Clipboards and notebooks.
Maps.
A digging area.

What you do:
Make up a story about digging in the garden and striking something really interesting with your spade. Go on to explain how you gently uncovered something really interesting…how you cleaned away the earth to reveal your treasure…and then show the children what you found. Show them some pictures of archaeologists searching for clues and talk about why they do this work and why it is important. Introduce the children to the materials in the box and show them where they can dig and how to record their findings. Once they are using the materials for themselves observe their play carefully to see what is capturing their interest. When the children are not around, bury some really interesting things for them to uncover in the digging area.

Further possibilities:
Make a visit to a local museum to view some things that have been discovered by archaeologists and then make an exhibition of some of the things uncovered by the archaeologists in your setting.

The Barbecue Box

What you need:
A small barbecue set.
Some charcoal.
Some cooking utensils.
Real or pretend food.
Plastic cups, plates and cutlery.
A tablecloth.
Recipe book of barbecue food.
Notebooks and pencils.

What you do:
Explore the contents of the box with the children and encourage them to talk about their own experiences of going to a barbecue. Watch carefully as they use the materials and be alert for ways in which you might extend the play through the addition of extra materials. Photograph the play at various points and use the photographs to help the children to recall and talk about their play. Share the recipe book with them and discuss the things they would most like to have at their barbecue.

Further possibilities:
When you have enough adult support, plan a proper barbecue. Involve the children in shopping for and preparing the food and encourage them to write and distribute invitations to the barbecue.

The Outdoor Café

What you need:
Chairs and tables, plates, cutlery and a variety of containers.
Aprons, notepads and pencils.
Food (real or pretend).
Tea towels and washing up bowls.
A blackboard and chalk for writing menus.
Open and closed signs.
Money and a till.
Garden umbrellas (if available).

What you do:
Talk with the children about the outdoor café and encourage them to offer their ideas about where it should be situated. (They may have additional ideas about what should be included in the resource list). Involve the children in arranging the resources in the agreed area and discuss what sort of food they think should be served in the café. Write their suggestions up on the menu board. (Once they have seen this modelled they will want to do the same). Consider holding an adult initiated session in the outdoor café as this will give you an opportunity to model how it can be used. Where possible, get some other adults to assist you. Young children learn by listening, watching and copying and when they see adults role-playing the behaviours of the cooks, waiters and customers, they want to do the same!

Further possibilities:
Arrange some 'special events' in the outdoor café, for example, a pizza day, a salad day, or you could serve food from a particular culture.

The Rapper's Box

What you need:
Some microphones.
A battery operated CD player.
Some action raps and other rap CDs. For example, 'Ros Bayley's Action Raps', 'Ros Bayley's Beanbag Raps', 'Keeping the Beat' CD (see Lawrence Educational website: www.LawrenceEducational.co.uk)
A selection of the children's favourite songs and action rhymes on CD.

What you do:
Introduce the children to The Rapper's Box as a focused activity. Talk about the contents of the box and model how it can be used. Show the children how to use the CD player and the microphones and ask for their suggestions for additional rhymes and raps that might be included in the box.

Further possibilities:
Help the children to make up some raps of their own and record them for future use and add them to The Rapper's box. Write out or word process the children's raps and include them in the box. Photocopy some of the raps and, once laminated, display them in the 'Performance Area.'

The Busker's Box

What you need:
An interesting collection of musical instruments and some 'song sheets' featuring a range of familiar songs.
Some photographs of different types of buskers.
A baton for the conductor.

What you do:
Talk through the possible uses of the Busker's Box. For example, they might set up a 'bandstand' in an appropriate part of the outdoor area, or they may prefer to have a 'marching band' or a choir. Share the pictures of different sorts of buskers and encourage the children to share their own experiences of seeing music played outside. Once you have done this, watch carefully to see how the children prefer to use the materials, and support accordingly.

Further possibilities:
Put on some special performances in the outside area. You could have a special noticeboard giving details of performances and the times they are to take place. If the children become really confident you might even consider doing some busking around other areas of the setting or in the local community.

The Explorer's Box

What you need:
Maps, binoculars, cameras, compass, water bottles, notebooks, pencils, sketch books, torches, picnic set, drapes, string and pegs for making dens.

What you do:
Talk with the children about what it means to become an explorer. Encourage them to think about where they would like to go exploring and talk about the things they will need for survival. Introduce them to the contents of the box and ask them if they think there is anything else they will need. Once you have done this observe their play carefully to see how it develops. Where appropriate, help them to extend the narrative around their exploration and add any materials that will assist them. Encourage them to photograph their exploration as it takes place and show them how they can use the notebooks and sketchbooks to record their adventures.

Further possibilities:
Change some of the contents of the box to encourage different sorts of exploration e.g. a polar expedition, a space mission or a rain forest adventure! Keep a photographic record of the children's play and use the photographs as a basis for an explorer's journal.

The Building Site

What you need:
Hard hats.
Buckets and spades.
Tool kits.
Nails and screws.
Building plans.
Tape measures and rulers.
Wooden blocks, planks and large blocks.
Pulleys, guttering, ropes etc.
Milk crates, bread crates and other suitable boxes.
Clipboards and pens.
Signs e.g. HARD HATS TO BE WORN IN ALL AREAS.
Collection of books about building e.g. Bob the Builder.

What you do:
Prior to setting up this activity look to see if there is any building work taking place in your local area. If there is, take the children on regular visits to observe it so that they can develop ideas to integrate into their play. (If this is possible it will really enhance this activity.)
Tape off part of the outside area as the building site. (It is a good idea to include a climbing frame within this area as this can act as a basis for the building and can also be used to explore pulleys.) If you can acquire some building plans, share these with the children and then talk with them about the sort of structure they would like to build. Help them to draw up their own plans. You might even suggest they need to apply for planning permission.

Further possibilities:
Photograph the building or structure in its various stages and use the photographs as the basis for a book. You could also video the proceedings and use the video as a basis for review and discussion.

Poetry For All Seasons

What you need:
Some poetry anthologies.
People's memories.
Card or paper.
Laminating equipment.

What you do:
Search for as many 'outdoor' poems as you can find. This may include poems from anthologies that practitioners or other adults in the setting learned as children and can still remember.

Type and print out each poem onto a separate strong piece of paper or card. Add the children's illustrations and laminate. Punch a hole in the top left hand corner and add a loop of string or similar, so that the poems can be hung outside for use at an appropriate moment.

You might wish to make collections that fit with different types of weather- poems about the rain for example, or the wind. Make a taped anthology of children reciting their favourites. Use in the listening corner inside.

Further possibilities:
Broaden your collection to include playground songs and games. Use them with the children and take photographs. Compile as an anthology for use outside.

The Seaside

What you need:
A paddling pool.
A pile of sand.
Buckets & Spades.
Rubber Rings.
An ice-cream stall.
A gift / souvenir stall.
Some books about the seaside.
Shells, plastic sea creatures etc.
A groundsheet (optical).

What you do:
Fill the paddling pool with water and arrange the sand around it.
Talk with the children about the things they would like on the souvenir and the ice-cream stalls, and help them collect the necessary resources.
Make price lists.
Discuss whether they think they will need any additional signs, for example, 'LIFEGUARD', 'DANGER', 'Don not go beyond this point' etc.
If you need to keep your 'seaside' contained within boundaries set the whole thing up on a groundsheet or tarpaulin.

Further possibilities:
Take photographs of the children as they play in the 'seaside' area and use them to make a 'holiday album'.
Talk with the children about the photographs and encourage them to think about suitable captions.
If you have a puppet area outside, consider integrating it into the seaside role-play as a Punch & Judy Show.

Children's books mentioned in the text:

Harry and the Dinosaurs Romp in the Swamp by Ian Whybrow, illustrated by by Adrian Reynolds

The Gruffalo by Julia Donaldson,

The Green Ship by Quentin Blake

Come Away from the Water Shirley by John Burningham

Room on the Broom by Julia Donaldson

Duck in the Truck by Jez Alborough

Where the Wild Things Are by Maurice Sendak

We're Going on a Bear Hunt by Michael Rosen and Helen Oxenbury

Whatever Next! by Jill Murphy

Billy's Bucket by Kes Gray and Garry Parsons

Where's Julius? by John Burningham

Owl Babies by Martin Waddell

Ros Bayley's Action Raps by Ros Bayley, Lawrence Educational

Ros Bayley's Beanbag Raps by Ros Bayley, Lawrence Educational

Several different versions of The Three Billy Goats Gruff

Several different versions of The Gingerbread Man

The Bob the Builder stories

CDs mentioned in the text:

Ros Bayley's Action Raps CD by Ros Bayley, Lawrence Educational

Ros Bayley's Beanbag Raps CD by Ros Bayley, Lawrence Educational

Keeping the Beat Nursery Rhymes CD by Keeping the Beat

We hope you have found this publication useful. Other titles in our 'Exciting Things To Do' series are:

BUILDER'S TRAY	50 ways to use a Builder's Tray	978-1-903670-15-6
LET'S EXPLORE	50 starting points for science activities	978-1-903670-11-8
LET'S BUILD	50 exciting ideas for construction play	978-1-903670-30-9
LET'S MOVE & DANCE	50 exciting starting points for Music & Dance	978-1-903670-35-4
LET'S WRITE	50 starting points for writing experiences	978-1-903670-10-1
LITERACY OUTDOORS	50 starting points for outdoor literacy experiences	978-1-903670-53-8
MATHS OUTDOORS	50 exciting ways to develop mathematical awareness	978-1-903670-61-3
MATHS THROUGH STORIES	50 exciting ideas for developing maths through stories	978-1-903670-46-0
NURSERY RHYMES	50 nursery rhymes to play with	978-1-903670-23-1
OUTSIDE	50 exciting things to do outside	978-1-903670-07-1
PICTURE THIS	50 ways to use a camera in early years settings	978-1-903670-22-4
PLANT AN IDEA	50 exciting ways to use flowers, trees and plant life	978-1-903670-24-8
SCIENCE OUTDOORS	50 exciting ideas for outdoor science activities	978-1-903670-67-5
SMALL WORLD RECIPE BOOK	50 exciting ideas for small world play	978-1-903670-39-2
STORYBOXES	50 exciting ideas for small world play	978-1-903670-39-2
STORYLINES	50 ideas for using large puppets, dolls & soft toys	978-1-903670-06-4
SUPERHEROES & POPULAR CULTURE	50 exciting ideas for using superheroes & popular culture	978-1-903670-79-8

For details on these and all our other early years resources visit our website: www.LawrenceEducational.co.uk